The History Of Popular Education On The Western Reserve: An Address

Burke Aaron Hinsdale

In the interest of creating a more extensive selection of rare historical book reprints, we have chosen to reproduce this title even though it may possibly have occasional imperfections such as missing and blurred pages, missing text, poor pictures, markings, dark backgrounds and other reproduction issues beyond our control. Because this work is culturally important, we have made it available as a part of our commitment to protecting, preserving and promoting the world's literature. Thank you for your understanding.

THE HISTORY OF POPULAR EDUCATION ON THE WESTERN RESERVE.

AN ADDRESS DELIVERED IN THE SERIES OF EDUCATIONAL CONFERENCES HELD IN ASSOCIATION HALL, CLEVELAND, SEPTEMBER 7 AND 8, 1896.

BY A. HINSDALE, PH. D., LL. D., PROFESSOR OF THE SCIENCE AND THE ART OF TEACHING IN THE UNIVERSITY OF MICHIGAN.

It is peculiarly appropriate that the programme of the Centennial Commemoration of the founding of the City of Cleveland and of the beginnings of the Western Reserve should embrace a generous recognition of the subject of education. It is fitting also that the conferences that mark this recognition should come at or near the close of the commemoration season rather than at the beginning, suggesting, as the fact does, the relation that education bears to all that has gone before. Nothing is more honorable to the Reserve than the prominence of education in its history. Nothing has given more character to its people than their educational intelligence, zeal, and activity. In nothing can they more confidently challenge comparison with other communities than in their devotion to schools and learning. In fact, the Reserve was twice dedicated to education, — once by the General Assembly of Connecticut, and once by the people that have made its history. While the history of the first dedication belongs to Connecticut rather than to Ohio, it will not be unfitting briefly to recite it as a prologue to the main discourse.

The reservation by the State of Connecticut, in 1786, of the block of territory to which the names Connecticut Reserve, New Connecticut, and Western Reserve were soon applied, raised at once the question, What shall be done with it? Several answers were returned to this question before the right one was finally found.

In October of the year just named, a month after the Connecticut cession, the General Assembly passed an act that authorized the survey and sale of a portion of the Reserve, with a proviso that five hundred acres of land in every township should be reserved for the support of the ministry, and the same quantity for the support of schools, within the township. This act was premature; only 24,000 acres were sold under it and it was repealed. In May, 1793, the half million acres lying across the Western end of the Reserve were given to the inhabitants of eight Connecticut towns who had suffered loss of property in the British raids into the State in the Revolutionary War. These lands, known as the Sufferers' Lands in Connecticut, and as the Fire Lands in Ohio, comprise Huron and Erie counties. In October of the same year the Assembly authorized the sale of the remaining lands on certain terms and conditions, and at the same time enacted: "That the moneys arising from the sale. . . . . be established a perpetual fund, the interest whereof is granted and shall be appropriated to the use and benefit of the several ecclesiastical societies, churches, or congregations of all denominations in the State to be by them applied to the support of their respective ministers or preachers of the Gospel and schools of education, under such rules and regulations as shall be adopted by this or some future session of the General Assembly." This provision at once created a violent agitation throughout the State, in the course of which the ecclesiastical societies and ministers of the Gospel came in for the lion's share of the public attention. The people of one town, in public meeting, declared that the appropriation was a step towards establishing a permanent sacerdotal order, and this opinion was more or less generally entertained. A still earlier proposition had been to devote the lands wholly to the support of the Connecticut ministry. This agitation went on for two years, but in the meantime the lands were not sold.

In May, 1795, the Assembly passed a new act, repealing the old one and making new terms of sale. At the same time the Assembly put the controversy about the disposition to be made of the proceeds at rest. It constituted these proceeds a perpetual fund, the interest of which should be applied to the support of schools within the State, according to the provisions of law then existing or from time to time enacted. A few months later the lands were sold to the Connecticut Land Company, and the payments, as they were made, were applied as the law directed. Moreover, the interest was capitalized until the fund amounted to about two million dollars. Such was the origin of the Connecticut Common School Fund, which, in the boyhood of men now living, was celebrated in the school geographies as one of the glories of American civilization. This fund still exists in its integrity, for the State watches over it with scrupulous care; but it has paled its ineffectual fires before the far greater school funds of later times.

It has been seen that at first Connecticut proposed to make a generous endowment for education on the Reserve soil. For some reason she abandoned this idea; she appropriated the soil to her own exclusive benefit, at the same time that her children by thousands were flocking to New Connecticut, where they were left to provide themselves with schools and education as best they could.

Briefly told this is the story of the first dedication of the Western Reserve to education. It was a dedication in a very literal sense of the term. The story of the second dedication, which was a far greater achievement, it will take much longer to tell.

The History of Popular Education in Ohio may be divided into three periods, as follows:

1. The period extending from the planting of the first settlements in 1788 to the enacting of the first general school law in 1821.

2. The period extending from 1821 to the reorganization and expansion of the school system of the State in 1853.

3. The period extending from 1853 to the present time.

These may be called the periods of preparation, planting, and development. To fill out this outline would be quite beyond the possibilities of the hour; but enough may be said to render it intelligible.

The Land Ordinance of 1785, the contracts that Congress made with the Ohio Company and with Symmes and his associates in 1787, and the Enabling Act of 1802 for the admission of the State to the Union, with exceptions soon to be noted, gave the inhabitants of every Congressional Township in Ohio Section No. 16, or one thirty-sixth part of the whole township, for the use of schools. Another act of legislation vested the title of these lands in the State Legislature. But these acts had no application to three extensive divisions of the State; viz.: The Western Reserve, the Virginia Military District, and the United States Military Bounty Lands, amounting to one-third of the whole area. Connecticut, as we have seen, had appropriated to her own use the whole of her reservation, and so had Virginia. The result was that the people of these three divisions were at a disadvantage compared with the people of the other parts of the State. Congress, however, by a series of acts came generously to their relief, appropriating them lands within the State, but beyond their own borders, that put them on the same footing as their neighbors. Thus, in 1807, Congress gave the Reserve eighty-seven and one-half square miles of school lands in the present counties of Tuscarawas and Holmes, and fifty-nine square miles more in 1834 in the northwestern part of the State, making one hundred and forty-six and one-half square miles, or 93,760 acres, in all. The school lands of the whole State amounted to eleven or twelve hundred square miles of surface, not including the three townships that were granted for Universities.

There is little reason to think that the framers of the Constitution of 1802 contemplated a school system to be supported by the State. All they did for education was to put into Article VIII of the Constitution the three following sections:

"Sec. 3. Religion, morality, and knowledge, being essentially necessary to the good government and the happiness of mankind, schools and the means of instruction shall forever be encouraged by legislative provision, not inconsistent with the rights of conscience."

"Sec. 25. No law shall be passed to prevent the poor in the several counties and townships within this State from an equal participation in the schools, academies, colleges, and universities within this State which are endowed in whole or in part from the revenue arising from the donations made by the United States for the support of schools and colleges; and the doors of the said schools, academies, and universities shall be open for the reception of scholars, students, and teachers of every grade, without any distinction or preference whatever, contrary to the intent for which the said donations were made."

"Sec. 27. Every association of persons, when regularly formed, within this State, and having given themselves a name, may, on application to the Legislature, be entitled to receive letters of incorporation, to enable them to hold estates, real and personal, for the support of their schools, academies, colleges, universities, and other purposes."

And this was all. The late Dr. Eli T. Tappan, one of the foremost educators that the State has produced, who investigated the subject with great care, said it was doubtful whether anything more was contemplated by the framers in regard to schools than the granting of corporate powers and the protecting of rights of person and property. The framers seem to have believed, he says further, that the school lands, including the university lands, would be adequate for the support of schools, academies, colleges, and universities. However this may be, all legislation relative to a public school system down to 1821 dealt with the school lands only. Touching this legislation, it will suffice to say that the General Assembly first attempted to lease the lands, and, that plan failing, finally offered them for sale, and in due time they were all sold. This was the source of the Irreducible School Fund of the State, which amounts to about three and a half million dollars. The last of the Reserve lands were sold in 1852. The portion of the whole State Fund that belongs to the Reserve is something more than a quarter of a million dollars. These results seem small; but we must remember that the problem of handling school lands in great quantities was a new one, that Ohio was the first State to grapple with it, and that, in those days, wild lands were more abundant than buyers.

In the first of the three periods, the General Assembly did very little for education. It legislated concerning the two universities at Athens and Oxford: beyond this it did nothing except to authorize school companies. All education previous to 1821 was purely voluntary, — as voluntary in provision as it was in attendance. Associated effort was of course resorted to where schools were established, for in the Ohio wilderness there were few families who could keep a private teacher. Citizens living within permitting distances would naturally act together in the provision and maintenance of schools for their children. School houses would be furnished and teachers employed. In such a state of affairs, charters of incorporation would often become desirable, if not necessary. Accordingly, acts incorporating schools begin to appear in the Statute book as early as 1808, and in 1817 a general act was passed to provide for the incorporation of school and library companies. Such companies were authorized to own property valued at ten thousand dollars, but were forbidden, on pain of forfeiting their charters, to employ any portion of their funds for banking purposes. How generally the schools took advantage of this legislation, and how generally they remained mere private associations, it would not be easy to ascertain.

In January, 1821, the General Assembly passed an act to provide for the regulation and support of common schools. This act authorized the division of townships into school districts, the election by the householders of the districts of school committees, the acceptance by these committees of gifts of land for school house sites, and the taxation of the property of all residents in the districts that were subject to State or county taxation for the purpose of erecting school houses, and also for the purpose of making up any deficiency that might accrue by the schooling of children whose parents or guardians were unable to pay for the same. The amount of taxes so levied in any district should not exceed one-half the amount levied for State or county purposes. The school committees were authorized to employ competent teachers, and to assess the expenses of the schools on the parents or guardians of all scholars in proportion to the whole number of scholars attending, provided that they might remit the assessments, in whole or part, made on parents or guardians who were unable to pay them. The committee might buy lots for school purposes if none were given or purchased by subscription. Every school in a township should have its proportion of rents arising from the school lands.

Such are the salient features of the first Ohio general school law. The law calls for a few words of comment. In the first place, its language is permissive merely, not mandatory: it authorizes the doing of a few things, but commands the doing of nothing. In the next place, it authorizes taxation for but two purposes — to provide school houses and to pay the fees of children whose parents are too poor to pay them. This is a suggestion of the so-called pauper schools, of which we hear more in some of the other States than in Ohio. Not a word is said about fuel, furniture, or incidental expenses. It is assumed that the people who use the schools will meet the major part of the expense directly, without any reference to the tax collector. The property of non-residents is not to be taxed for school purposes. The voluntary principle, it may be observed, was counted on by the General Assembly long after this time. Taxation for school furniture and fuel was not authorized until 1838; the school bill as a means of partially paying teachers lingered until 1853, and the good old plan of boarding around, which was a device for lengthening out the school money, perhaps still lingers in some parts of the State. How generally the people availed themselves of the powers of the act of 1821, we cannot tarry to inquire. Nor can we or need we follow step by step the evolution of the school system of which it was the beginning. Still, some of the more important facts cannot be omitted.

In 1825 the General Assembly passed a new law, which differed from the previous one in two important particulars. First, it was written in the language of command. It shall be the duty of the auditor, of the trustees, of the school directors, etc., the sections run. The new style suggests, what was no doubt true, that the people, as ministers say in relation to another subject, had not lived up to their privileges. A mere permission to educate conferred by law never yet produced a good school system. Selfishness is always strong enough to defeat general education on that basis. Experience has proved conclusively that three things are essential to an educated state: The provision of schools must be made obligatory; tuition must be practically free, and attendance upon the schools must be compulsory. The other change in the new law was the much wider range of powers conferred. The very first section provided for raising funds by taxation for the use of common schools, but not to exceed one-half a mill on the dollar. Boards of County Examiners were provided for, and only certificated persons could be employed as teachers. From this time forward there was a State fund available for the payment of teachers; but until 1853 it was never large enough, unless in favored localities, to permit the disuse of the rate bill.

The two laws of 1821 and 1825 were secured largely through the efforts of Judge Ephraim Cutler, of Washington county. It is soberly written in history that in 1825 there was in the Legislature a "school" party and a "canal" party; the first wanted schools, and the second canals, but neither one could secure a majority for its favorite measure; so the two parties worked together, and, as a result, won both schools and canals. The fact shows how times have changed; the proposition to connect the fortunes of the public schools and of the canals of Ohio at the present day would be ludicrous indeed.

From 1825 onward the State, participating in the general educational movement of the country, continued to make slow but steady progress. Sometimes a step was lost, but it was soon regained. It was the day of the common school revival. The Constitution of 1851 marks a great advance on 1802. Besides throwing its shield over the State School Fund, and casting a bulwark about the treasury to turn aside sectarian assaults, the new instrument declares: "The General Assembly shall make such provisions, by taxation or otherwise, as, with the income arising from the school trust fund, will secure a thorough and efficient system of common schools throughout the State." The act of 1853 entitled "An Act to provide for the reorganization, supervision, and maintenance of common schools", was the speedy fulfillment of this promise. This law provided an augmented school fund, established a central education office at the State capital, strengthened local authorities, and gave to common schools an impulse that they have never lost.

A few words touching the third period will answer the present purpose. The progress that the State has made in education is very great indeed. A few statistics will tell the story. In 1854 the pupils reported enrolled in the schools were 456,191. In 1895 the number was 817,490. The average attendance for the two years was 277,196 and 593,465 pupils. The school year had also considerably increased in length. The high school attendance at the first date was 4,611; at the second date 48,390. The total expenditure for public schools in 1854 was $2,266,457. In 1895, not counting interest on bonds redeemed, it was $12,496,345. The average pay per month of male teachers has nearly doubled, of female teachers considerably more than doubled. Still it must be said that the statistics are much more full and accurate now than they were then.

In no feature that strikes the eye has the improvement been so great as in school houses. Marvelous is hardly too strong a word to describe the change. In the year 1850 there were ten or more district school houses in the township of Wadsworth, Medina county, all well filled with pupils when the winter school was in session. I was familiar with the exterior of nearly all of these buildings, and with the interior of three or four of them. It would be quite safe to say that there was not a building among the number that to-day would sell for one hundred dollars. The one that I knew best was clapboarded and shingled, but there was not a bit of mortar about it, save what had been put into the chimney; while a Webster's "Elementary Spelling Book" could have been passed from the inside to the outside without opening the door or raising a window. But it would be a mistake to suppose that this district was behind others in enterprise.

Three Ohio men now deceased have exercised a far-reaching influence upon popular education throughout the country, and one of these belongs to the Reserve. These men were known in quite different ways. William H. McGuffey was little more than McGuffey's Readers, and Joseph Ray little more than Ray's Arithmetics and Algebras. But Thomas W. Harvey, in Ohio at least, was much more than Harvey's Grammars. This is not the place to recount at length Mr. Harvey's personal or educational history. As teacher and superintendent at Chardon, Republic, Massillon, and Painesville, as State Examiner and Commissioner of Common Schools, and as institute lecturer, he gained, it is probable, a wider personal knowledge of the teachers and schools of the State than any other man of his time. He was a charter member of the State Association, and for more than forty years was closely identified with every forward educational movement in the State. If not the greatest scholar or pedagogical thinker of the circle in which he moved, he was a good scholar and thinker; while his companionable ways, wisdom in council, long experience, sense of honor, and devotion to his chosen calling drew men to him wherever he went. All things considered, it may be doubted whether any other man has left a stronger impress on public education in Ohio than Thomas Harvey.

Let it not be supposed that I have forgotten the subject. The historical outline that has been drawn embraces the Western Reserve as well as the other parts of the State. Still from the beginning until 1853 the Reserve more than participated in the great educational advance that was made: She often led the column. Some examples of this leadership may be mentioned.

Previous to 1853 special school laws were often passed for particular localities. This was permissible under the old Constitution. Perhaps the best of these laws, and the one most widely copied, was the Akron law, enacted in 1847. This law now seems to us a very simple matter, but it was a great matter in its time. It was enacted in response to a popular demand that was led by the Rev. Mr. Jennings, at the time pastor of the Congregational church of Akron. The law made the town one school district, created one school board of six members, authorized a suitable number of primary schools and one central grammar school, and conferred power to levy taxes sufficient to meet the expense of the system. It has been said that the State law of 1853 was little more than an amplification of the Akron law. Under this law the late General M. D. Leggett organized the schools of Akron as superintendent, for which service he received the munificent salary of five hundred dollars a year. In 1847 Akron witnessed another interesting event. This was the organization of the Ohio State Teachers' Association, which has exercised such an important influence upon education in the State. Not only was the Association organized on the soil of the Reserve, but the meeting was called and the organization effected mainly through the efforts of Western Reserve men. Again, the first teachers' institute ever held in the West was held on the Reserve. The place was Sandusky, the year 1845. And, once more, Cleveland joined hands with Cincinnati to secure the school law of 1853. This act was carried through the Legislature by the Hon. Harvey Rice, then a senator from Cuyahoga county. And, generally, it will be found that the men of the Reserve were at the fore when there was an opportunity to do anything for schools and education.

Books of chronicles, while dry and uninteresting to most people, are full of marrow and fatness to those who have been touched by the historical passion. The educational chronicles of the Reserve in the early days are scanty, but eloquent for that very reason. We shall look into some of these books. And first a little volume called "Memoirs of Rev. Joseph Badger."

Father Badger, first of the missionaries sent to New Connecticut by the Connecticut Missionary Society, reached Poland at the end of December, 1800. The oldest Reserve settlements were but three years old, and the total population was 1302. Badger spent several years in missionary work in the Northeastern part of the State, commonly making his home in Austinburg. He relates that he found three families at Cleveland in June, 1801, and that he assisted in organizing the first church on the Reserve, at Austinburg, in October of the same year. Badger was a college man, and, as he revolved in his mind the question of removing his family to the Western wilderness, he reflected: "Our family of six children must now be taken from school to grow up in the woods without any advantage of even a common school for years." Occasionally he speaks of visiting a school. Early in 1803 we meet this entry: "Visited a school of sixteen children, the first attempted in this place." The place was, apparently, Austinburg. A year later he speaks of preaching in the North School House, Harpersfield, language which seems to imply a South School House also. As late as April 8, 1810, he wrote: "By preaching in different settlements, and visiting all schools now beginning to be set up, I learned the great want of school books, and by family visits I also learned the want of suitable books in families." Accordingly Badger, forming an Eastern connection for that purpose, undertook to supply both wants, in which he confesses he was not very successful.

Rev. Thomas Robbins, D. D., was the second missionary sent to the Reserve by the Connecticut Society. He arrived in December, 1803, and returned in May, 1806. His particular field of labor was Trumbull and Mahoning counties, but, like Badger, he traveled over the whole eastern half of the Reserve. While

Robbins' diary, consisting of more than two thousand octavo pages, covering fifty-six years of life, is as dull a book of its kind as could well be written, the two hundred pages covering his experience in New Connecticut contains many an interesting item. In the course of his journeyings he speaks of schools twenty or more times. Generally his mention is the mere fact, "Visited a school"; but sometimes he adds a word of comment, as that the school was small, or poorly governed but ambitious, or was well instructed, particularly in the catechism. He saw the frame of the first Burton academy in December, 1804, and was urged to become its first head, and the minister of the church.

Persons who are familiar with New England history will not be surprised to learn that a movement was on foot in those early days to found a college in New Connecticut. Both Badger and Robbins mention it several times. Boards of trustees were elected, sites were canvassed, and an act of incorporation was secured while Ohio was still a part of the Northwest Territory. Robbins mentions that one prospectus was sent to Connecticut to be printed. These efforts at college building were tentative only; still they point forward to Western Reserve College, founded at Hudson in 1826.

It is to be hoped that none grow weary of these old chronicles, or think them trivial. They are not dead but living; as was said of the words used by a great master of speech, cut them and they will bleed. We are standing at the sources of a great history, and we need not be in haste to descend the stream. We are not dealing with the smart new brick school house that stands on the main street in the village; or with the little red school house that stands in the country at the crossing of the roads; but with the old log school house that stood in the edge of the clearing which, with strong hands, was chopped out of the forest. Things have changed mightily since Hooker and Davenport made their plantings at Hartford and New Haven early in the seventeenth century; but in the thirst for education and zeal for schools the Connecticut stock have not changed. These chronicles tell us that, almost before the surveyors were out of the woods, the little communities sprinkled here and there through the wilderness were doing what they could to meet present educational needs and to plant for the future. It was, indeed, a day of small things; but in these small things lay the potency of the century that has now come to a close.

The chronicles of education often touch the heart and cause the lip to quiver. There is often pathos in the efforts that young men and women make to obtain mental culture, whether they are made in pioneer schools or in great universities. Take the story of Platt R. Spencer, the teacher and author, who traveled twenty miles and back again on foot to borrow a copy of Daboll's Arithmetic; or of Joshua R. Giddings, the statesman, who, denied the privileges of education after he was a small boy, never thought that he could have a profession until he was twenty-three years old, when he went regularly to school to a Presbyterian minister residing in the same town; or of Samuel Bissell, the minister and educator, who walked from Portage county to New Haven carrying his pack on his back, that he might study at Yale College.*

In the pioneer days we come upon no trace of a character who is familiar in many of the Southern States and in parts of Ohio. I refer to the Scotch-Irish schoolmaster. The New Connecticut Yankees had no use for him. The teachers of those days were not itinerants, but resident members of the several communities. They worked for small pay, and often received this in forms that would embarrass the modern schoolmaster or schoolma'am. Thus, the late Peter Hitchcock, of Burton, taught a winter's school in Burton and received his pay in pork and provisions. The Presbyterian and Congregational ministers did good educational service in those days, sometimes teaching the schools and sometimes private scholars in their own homes.

It would be inexcusable to omit from this summary the academies of the early time. The first of these schools, and one of the best, was the Burton Academy, opened to scholars in the winter of 1806-7. The building was 25 x 50; two school rooms and a hallway below, and a room for a church above. This structure burned in 1810, and was replaced with a more commodious one in 1819. It is said that the first term boys attended who lived

---

*Dr. Julian M. Sturtevant's *Autobiography* edited by J. M. Sturtevant, Jr., gives an interesting account of the manner in which some Ohio boys (1822-1826) obtained a college education. Fleming Revell Co., N. Y., Chicago, Toronto.

at a distance of five and six miles, which they doubled on foot twice every day. This academy flourished and narrowly escaped expanding into a college. "Students came in from every direction," says the local chronicler; "The Tods and Wickses from Youngstown, the Austins and Hawleys from Austinburg, the Perkinses and others from Warren." Another celebrated school of the same kind was founded at Norwalk in 1826. One authority pronounces this the largest and most famous institution of the kind in all the West. Here President Hayes, Governor Foster, General McPherson, and many others who attained a good degree, studied. Edward Thomson, afterwards president of Ohio Wesleyan University, and a bishop of the Methodist Episcopal Church, was at one time the principal. This school also narrowly escaped becoming a college; but as Burton had its Hudson, so Norwalk had its Delaware.

It must not be supposed that these schools of higher grade were few in number. The fact is they were many. At some time previous to 1850 nearly every enterprising township had its academy, or at least its select school, and, collectively, these schools exercised a prodigious influence upon society. The best of them were regularly incorporated institutions, owning their own property. They drew within their walls the ambitious sons and daughters of the most cultivated families, and often attracted students from a considerable distance. The Wadsworth Academy, taught by John McGregor, who had studied at the University of Edinburg, called students from Cleveland, Canton, and Millersburg. The teachers were often scholarly men. While these schools did much elementary teaching, as we should esteem it, they also did much real secondary work. The Brahman families of Northeastern Ohio towns sent their sons to Burton Academy to be fitted for Yale College.

These higher schools explain how it was that the Western Reserve became a nursery for school teachers. The supply was in excess of the local demand, and many young men wandered away to the southern part of the State or to other States in search of employment as teachers. Young James Garfield went to Muskingum county on such an errand. The veteran Judge Lester Taylor, of Claridon, speaking of Geauga county, once said: "Every township has more or less kept up schools for the benefit of advanced scholars, to study higher branches, during winter months. From all classes of these schools there has been graduated a class of qualified teachers, largely in excess of the home demand, who have for the last forty years gone south and west to teach in the winter, leaving in the fall as uniformly as the wild geese and other migratory birds, and returning to spend the summer in labor."

As the public schools increased in number and improved in quality, the academies began to lose ground. Wholly dependent, as a rule, on tuition charges for existence, they could not compete with free schools of equal grade. The law of 1853 gave them the finishing stroke. Some of the buildings were sold to boards of education, and many of the teachers entered the public schools; some of the old schools struggled bravely for existence, but in time nearly all, if not indeed all, of them passed into history.

There are two reasons for mentioning another celebrated school, which will appear in the sequel. The Western Reserve Teachers' Seminary opened its doors to the public in September, 1839, being established in the upper stories of the Temple at Kirtland, Lake county, which the Mormons had abandoned a short time before when they left the "First Stake" for the far West. This seminary existed about twenty years, and for much of the time was a very flourishing school. It drew to itself, as teachers and students, a number of persons who made a name in the world. Its foundation was mainly due to the efforts of the Rev. Nelson Slater, who served as first superintendent or principal. Dr. A. D. Lord was the head of this school for several years before he went to Columbus, and with him were associated M. F. Cowdery, Alfred Holbrook, and other well-known teachers. T. W. Harvey came from the printing office at Painesville, and M. D. Leggett from the farm in Montville, to study at Kirtland. Leggett was also employed for a time as one of the teachers. The other fact for which the seminary is noteworthy is the great attention that it paid to the preparation of teachers of both sexes for the common schools. In this respect it far surpassed any school on the Reserve that had gone before it, and, relatively speaking, it has perhaps not been equalled by any school that has succeeded it. It was founded only two years after the first Normal School in the United States was established, that at Lexington, Massachusetts.

In dealing with the Reserve I have been dealing with Cleveland. The majority of men are so little gifted with imagination, or are so poorly instructed in history, that they continually assume that all things continue as they were from the beginning. It is a very great mistake. In respect to education Cleveland is in no way marked off from other towns and villages until in quite recent times. The city merely repeats the history of Youngstown, Akron, and other places, only it has come to do things on a much larger scale. We can, therefore, run over the Cleveland story somewhat hastily.

Tradition tells of a school of five pupils in Cleveland when there were but three families on the ground. Who taught this school, as well as its exact date, cannot be told. We hear nothing more on the subject until 1814, when a school taught by a Mr. Chapman is mentioned: *Vox et preterca nihil*. In 1817, when the population had grown to two hundred and fifty, a school house was built on the lot now occupied by the Kennard House; just how it was built, it is hard to say. This was undoubtedly the first school house built on the site of Cleveland, unless there may have been an earlier one at Newburg or some other of the numerous centres that have been swallowed up by the growth of the city. In this school house children were taught on the payment of tuition fees. The Cleveland Academy, afterwards called the Old Academy, was built by subscription on St. Clair street in 1821. There is no trace of a public school system until the granting of the city charter. The trustees do not appear to have exercised the powers conferred by the acts of 1821 and 1825. The only schools were private schools.

The late S. H. Mather, in a published document, states that in 1833 or 1834 an attempt was made to organize a mission sunday school in the Bethel church; that the children were found so ignorant that proper sunday school teaching was out of the question; and that, to make good this deficiency, a day school was established to teach the children to read, the teacher being paid by voluntary subscription. This school, says Mr. Mather, was continued on this basis until the city, in 1835, assumed the charge of it and made it a city free school. So far as existing records show, the first public expenditure ever made for education in Cleveland was the cost of maintaining this school one year, $131.12. Not a large educational budget surely for a city that has come to expend something like a million dollars annually on its schools!

In 1836 Cleveland became a chartered city. The population was then five thousand. Two sections of the charter related to schools. The Common Council was authorized to levy a tax of not more than one mill on the dollar for the purchase of school sites and building school houses, and an additional mill for the support of a school in each of the three wards into which the city was divided, which should be accessible to all white children not under four years of age; the council should fix by ordinance the beginning and end of the school year, and appoint every year a board called the Board of Managers of the Common Schools, in which the particular administration should rest. This Board should make rules and regulations for the schools, examine and employ teachers, fix their salaries subject to the rules of the Council, make repairs of school houses and furnish supplies, and certify to the Council all expenses incurred in the performance of its duties. On July 7, 1837, the Common Council passed an ordinance in accordance with these sections of the charter, and this ordinance is the real beginning of public schools in Cleveland. The ordinance was drawn on the lines of the charter, only the school year was made four months instead of six. The schools were to provide only elementary education.

The Board of Education built its first public school houses, two in number, in 1839-40. In 1840 there were sixteen teachers and 1,040 pupils. The principal schools were divided into two departments, each department having a boys' school and a girls' school. An academical department, as it was called, or a high school as we should say, was opened in 1846, with Andrew Freese as principal. This school was opposed by some heavy tax payers, and it was never beyond danger until it was authorized by a special act of the Legislature, which came in 1848-49. The West Side High School, of which A. G. Hopkinson was the father, was opened in 1854. The training school went into operation in 1874.

The first superintendence that the schools received was given by a duly elected member of the Board of Managers, called the Acting Manager of the Schools. This form of superintendence lasted from 1841 to 1853. In the latter year Mr. Freese was elected Superintendent, and Dr. E. E. White succeeded him as the head of the High School. Mr. Freese was followed as superintendent by Mr. L. M. Oviatt, he by Rev. Anson Smythe, and he again by Mr. A. J. Rickoff. These gentlemen all devoted themselves with singleness of mind to the work of the schools, and all were rewarded by seeing the fruits of their labors. The pressing school questions of those years all over the country related to organization and system. The Cleveland history supports this view. Mr. Rickoff came to the superintendency in 1867 and held it until 1882. An educator of ripe experience and force of character, and the possessor of the confidence of a strong Board of Education for many years, he impressed himself deeply on the school system of the city. The existing organization is very largely his work. Under his direction the schools came to attract attention from far and near, and, in particular, they called out some glowing enconiums from foreign visitors.

Standing in the relation that it does to the Western Reserve, the City of Cleveland ought to lead in educational matters; and the other towns and cities would generally, if not universally, recognize the fact of such a leadership almost from the beginning of the union school movement.

At first the Board of Education was only a committee appointed by the City Council, but since 1859 it has been elected by the people at the popular election. Once more, the Board was wholly dependent upon the Common Council for funds until 1865; in that year it became fully autonomous, levying and expending its own revenues subject only to the law.

For many years there has been a growing conviction in many American cities, if not indeed in a majority of them, that the business administration of the public schools is getting, or rather has got, into a bad way. The trouble is thought to arise from the character of men who are often elected members of boards of education, from a vicious method of doing business, and from the nature of the business organization of the schools. At least this was the view taken by a great number of citizens of this city; for in response to a popular demand the Legislature passed, in 1892, the Reorganization Act, under which the schools are now carried on. I refer to this act with no purpose of discussing its provisions or of commenting on its operation. My aim is very different. The evils that it was intended to correct have become widespread; the act itself has attracted very general attention; in a sense, it is now on trial before the public, not of Cleveland alone, but of the country; and if experience shall finally prove that it accomplishes the end for which it was devised, Cleveland will become the teacher of the country in the important matter of city school administration.

One who attempts to write the educational history of a state or community is likely to commit the fault of confining himself too closely to professional educators. It is perfectly right that this class of persons should be emphatically recognized. But education has its business side as well as its pedagogical side. Teachers and superintendents alone, no matter how able and devoted, cannot make a school system. Educational discussions too much tend to run on professional lines. Accordingly, I wish to recognize in the heartiest manner the educational services to Ohio of such men as Ephraim Cutler, Rufus King, Samuel Lewis, Harvey Rice, and others; also the service to particular communities of such men as Charles Bradburn and George Willey, of this city, who not only served as members of the School Board for years, but actually did efficient duty as acting managers of the schools.

The decade 1835-45 is an important one in American educational history. It has been called our educational renaissance. In this period Massachusetts created the first State board of education, the first American normal school, and the first efficient State school superintendency, with Horace Mann in the office; Dr. Henry Barnard of Connecticut called the teachers' institute into being; New York established the first public school libraries; Michigan laid the foundation of her educational system on the lines of the Prussian ideas; the City of Providence, R. I., first established the local school superintendency. German influence now began to be felt by American scholars, teachers, and schools. The decade ushered in a period of school renovation, within and without. We shall form the best idea of this period by looking at it under a single phase and by limiting our view to Ohio.

It must be remembered that the largest cities of the State were once small villages, and that a single school answered all purposes. Time added scholars, and therefore called for new schools and new school districts. These schools and school districts were wholly separate and independent in organization and management. The educational world was without form and void and darkness was upon the face of the deep. Such legislation as the Akron school law was enacted to correct this state of things, and under it the organization of city and town schools commenced. The schools of Cincinnati were organized in 1840. The facts in regard to Cleveland have been already related. Dayton, Columbus, Akron, and other towns soon followed the example thus set. The law of 1853 gave the movement a great impulse. The name "union school" or "union schools" came into general use as expressing the prevailing tendency of the new time. If this name is now seldom heard, it is because the great work of unification in the city and town schools has been accomplished. Perhaps the new rural school movement will bring it into use again.

The union movement raised some difficult external problems for legislators, members of boards of education, and superintendents to solve. It also raised some internal problems that were even more difficult. The establishment of a system of grades and the classification of pupils now became a possibility. This possibility involved the evolution of a course of graded study, the adoption of canons and methods of promotion, and the provision of suitable text-books. These problems rested heavily on the hands of such men as Harvey, Henkle, Rickoff, and Cowdery for many years. Some people now believe, perhaps most people, that these problems were solved too successfully. Those who hold this view believe that too much stress came to be laid on system and uniformity. Considering the utter chaos that had reigned, together with the known tendency of the human mind to value machinery, this was in no way strange. Matters were sometimes carried to such a point that the schools of great cities were regularly halted once a month, that the children's minds might be examined, their contents inventoried and tabulated, and reports made to the superintendent's office, there to be compared and systematized. There is now a refluent tide. The peculiar work of that generation of educators has been accomplished, and we are now face to face with a new and a still more difficult series of problems. How shall we find room in our school system for freedom and spontaneity? How shall we adjust the individuality of the child to the necessity of school organization? These are some of the questions of the new era.

At the end of 1869 there was formed in this city the Northeastern Ohio Teachers' Association, which is still in vigorous life. It is not pertinent or necessary to enlarge on the history of this useful society. As soon as formed it plunged into the discussion of some of the most pressing questions of the time. In his inaugural address, Dr. Harvey, who was the first President of the Association, drew attention to several of these questions. He put first on his list a subject that, to my knowledge, has never seriously occupied the attention of the Association from that day to this. Reviewing the history of twenty years, he said while the schools in the towns and cities had made marked progress, and ranged among the best of their kind in the Union, those in the rural districts had not improved as they ought to have done. In some localities, he said, no progress whatever had been made. This subject is now beginning to claim the public attention, and there is some reason to think that we are on the eve of changes in the rural schools quite as striking as those that have been accomplished in the town and city schools. This topic may well be the last one to the treated in this address.

There are obvious difficulties in the way of bringing the country schools to as high a standard as the town and city schools, and it is by no means certain that it can ever be accomplished. Fortunately, however, there are some compensating advantages. One of these difficulties is the sparseness of rural population and the consequent insufficiency of pupils to be handled in the schools, which interferes with expansion and tends to repress interest and enthusiasm. This difficulty has been greatly intensified by the decline of population in many rural districts. For example, every decennial census since 1850 has shown a decline in the population of Geauga county. It is now about twenty-five per cent. less than it was at its maximum. Medina county also fell off for twenty years, but has slightly recovered itself at the last two censuses. Trumbull county lost two thousand five hundred people at the last census. Many townships in counties that have held their own in population, or even gained, have gone the same way. And so it is in many parts of the country: The last census showed that more than four hundred counties in the Union had lost population in ten years for other causes than reduction in size. These losses of population are an important factor, not only in education but also in religious and social life. Many schools once of good size, or even large, have become small; some have actually ceased to exist. Schools of two, three, and five pupils are by no means uncommon on the Reserve. My attention was first called to this subject about twenty-five years ago. A chart showing the size of the schools in different parts of the State prepared by Dr. T. C. Mendenhall formed part of the Ohio exhibit at Philadelphia in 1876. This chart made it very evident that, in this sense, not only parts of Ashtabula county, but parts of other counties, were "benighted." I publicly urged the consolidation of schools as a means necessary to correct the existing evil. Perhaps I may be pardoned for quoting a few sentences from an address that I delivered and published in 1878.

"Centralization is the only remedy for this state of things. There must be fewer school officers, fewer schools, fewer teachers, and more pupils in the schools. You cannot have a fire without fuel or a school without scholars. The Western Reserve Yankee is very conservative. Having always had a school house on the corner of his own or of his neighbor's farm, he cannot reconcile himself to the idea of sending his children three or four miles away. But in many places it must come to that in time; in such towns [as those mentioned] the children will be taught in consolidated schools or not at all. People will not long be so absurd as to keep up a district school for three scholars. When they make up their minds to the inevitable, which is in this case also the desirable, they will find that the necessary steps are both few and short.

It will be found both cheaper and better to carry the children to the distant school than to go on in the old way."

I now hear with no little satisfaction that the Reserve is beginning to move in this direction. The necessary legislation has been procured in several cases, and the schools of several towns have been more or less consolidated. Old buildings are abandoned if necessary and new ones built. The schools and teachers are much reduced in numbers and greatly improved in quality. A competent correspondent in Geauga county writes me as follows: "We carry the children to and from the school when necessary in closed hacks hired at public expense. We get the inspiration that comes from large numbers; we can classify according to advancement of the pupils; we are able to have a much better grade of teachers without any increase of taxes; we secure a more uniform attendance, and the children are never tardy; the instruction is at once better and cheaper." He adds that some people are opposed to the movement (people who are always opposed to new methods to meet changed conditions), but the opinion is spreading that the country district school does not measure up to the educational demands of the time.

This is progress. There is little more reason in having eight or ten district schools in a sparsely populated Ohio or Michigan township than there is in having an equal number of churches.

We have now taken a general survey of the large subject that was set for the hour. We have considered popular education on the Western Reserve, both in its general relations to the educational development of the State and in itself. However imperfect the treatment may have been, I hope the interest and dignity of the theme have at least been made apparent. How very creditable the record is to those who have made it! Nothing in their history does them greater honor. Born on the Reserve, of Connecticut stock; reared and educated here, and living here the greater part of my life; familiar with the history, conditions, and spirit of the people; proud of what has been accomplished on this soil, — I have counted it an honor to be called to participate in the observances that mark the close of one century of history and usher in a new one. Forgetting for the moment my removal from the State, and reasserting my rights as a child of the soil, I mingle my felicitations with yours, that we have behind us so glorious a history. We do well to recount the story of the past, — the sacrifices of the pioneers; the wisdom and constancy of the later founders; the fidelity of a great host of teachers; the educational zeal and intelligence of the public: but we do better resolutely to face the future, determine to do our own work as well as our predecessors have done theirs. If we and those who succeed us shall meet this high demand, then those who gather here a century hence to celebrate the second centennial of the founding of Cleveland and the beginnings of the Western Reserve will see

"Another morn
Risen on mid-noon."

Printed by Libri Plureos GmbH in Hamburg, Germany